FEMALE FANTASY

ITS IMPORTANT TO SMILE

NAGA UMA MAHESWARI
VEGURU

To Mom, Dad, Brother

Contents

Contents

Foreword

This book is the reflection of life. A mixture of dreams that lead me to the path of writing. I have been able to write this book because of my family. I thank my mom, dad, brother for always being my support system. This book is collection of poems which are framed from the experiences of my life. I hope this book fills encouragement in upcoming generations. I would like to thank notion press for giving me the opportunity to publish my book.

Naga Uma Maheswari Veguru.

Buchi Reddy Palem, Nellore

Preface

The thoughts are the right thread in the dark ages which brightened my life and gave me courage. I talk to myself that nothing is impossible. i believe in the truth rather than just the mere facts. The whole perspective of life changed right then.

Acknowledgements

I want to thank God for everything. I wish to contribute to society and its people. May the children of future and present take proper care of nature and cooperate in making components of nature valuable.

Prologue

It takes a great courage to choose the best over the worst.

1. Soul Story

And you know about me
I am intelligent, free, appealing soul
You observe the radinace of my smile
Do you recognize the smell of my sweat?
I awaken every morning
And I sit in my porch
I usually drink lemons with hot water
I glare at sun, birds, and the surrounding trees
There are plenty of banyan trees, coconut trees
There is calm
Coconut trees outreach to the sky like pillars
Four of them are adjacent to each other
And are playing with their big leaves open
It looks like a gentle magic
I feel like a queen while creating my own art kingdom
I am a girl who grew up enthusiastically
I feel young in my skin
Like a deep sea,
I conceal 90 percent of my thoughts
I strive to impress myself
But not others
I want to be a writer,
All I need is a typewriter,

enough food and sleep
a person who can accept me wholeheartedly
I want to have a flourishing life and relaxed frame of mind
I am here to welcome the world
To enlighten myself
To light up the world when it is dark
The star with me is beaming and shimmering
I believe I have had little luck over the years
And my luck was wonderful
It would be gratifying to become one great poet
As if washed properly in the machine,
I will elevate my luck parked in parking space
Luck is all mine, I value all the honor and desire
One day I will tell infront of the whole world how much I value it.

2. Bake It

Lioness doesn't really care about hyenas or wolves
I am a lioness
fire and mist sturdily wrapped in me
the glint of lionizing light
Watching myself grow from deep roots
That's where the heart shines in the gleam of sunlight
The true significance of light is emanated from the layers of darkness
I claim it "The equation of life"
Life is a cake, how you bake it is important
"Strawberry cake or chocolate cake?" asked a girl next to me , her eyes wide open
I smiled at her
She is my cousin Nilaya
I slowly took her hands in to mine saying,
"The flavor is your choice, make it tasty"
Make a delicious cake
Sometimes you may not be able to get the ingredients smoothly
Ride out of hard work
Build your empire, Health and wealth to you

3. Struggling for job

Reading computer science articles on Sunday afternoon
Seated on the tiny bed
I work day and night
Roaming around the college corridors to meet professors
To get approval of my project
It is said that as human beings we must fight
For things to sort out,
To live an undisturbed life
This turned out to be true
when the interview panel rejected me
I felt discouraged flumping into a chair
I was writing mawkish poems on success
For about half an hour
I lay down on the bed to take an instant nap
It seemed like a war in me
What's this life?
A nutshell framed in platinum
Waking up, eating, reading for a job
running from hostel mess to classroom
This literally looked like the engine was rumbling at 8:30 AM
And it must reach the platform by 10:00 PM
At this reading slump, the algorithms and pseudocodes become a nightmare

I read slowly, aloud
I keep writing bullet points
Over and over all day
Everytime I close the book after two hours and oh, what did I recite 2 minutes ago?
Whoops! What I had memorized all this time, melted like a butter
Even the girls and boys who never saw the face of the classroom were also recruited in companies
I smiled over all these thoughts
I signed into my laptop
To watch a movie
I paused and murmured "Good things take time
what can you do?
Just go and sit down and breathe"

4. This night

On a snowy midnight
Music is playing
The pack of dog's barking
Streetlight is beaming
Oh, life is so beautiful
Money can't buy calmness
In this perfect snowy weather
Watching the twig of maple leaves dance
What'd I do now?
I might read a book sitting on the sofa right at this moment of time
Love is pouring from stars
Tonight, snugging my big fella teddy bear
I tell the stars that this life is magical weave
Just dance for your own songs
That's where magic unfolds

5. Blessing

I see the sun,
The spirit of my soul is beaming
I see the Moon
The desire inside my heart is invigorating
I see the stars
The power of my thought is glittering
I watch the birds
self confidence is aroused
The universe is a real blessing
Scintallating sun's shine in every blush of forenoon
Flowers blossoming at times of spring
Bright stars are gleaming at night
Trees swaying in the wind bestow fruits, flowers, and oxygen
Air to inhale
Catering all the elements to live endlessly
Thankyou universe
We ought to protect you
we will not scuffle to take grip off your treasures
We walk in the right path
Thankyou for all the energy and joy

6. Dogs got No Rules

There is a rice mill in the middle of our street
Dogs are extremely ferocious and free
They have been barking all night
They are together on the mill premises
At night the owners lock the mill
There is a secret hole below the main door
These furry doggy fellas try to get into the street
Below the main entrance is a secret hole
Through this the dogs come out
Enjoying the nightlife
Snatching food on the streets
At first there is a big dog barking there,
This is called the 'leader'
Then the little dogs greet
They clap and cheer all night long
Giggling! Snarling!
Taking brisk walks, slick movements
They look keenly around every nook and corner
Clutching leftover food from polythene covers
Hurray….! Its delicious,
a little puppy jumps in joy singing "Dogs got no Rules"

7. Outta Style

These people are taught that way
They learn all of it and deliver it to future generations
They can't do poetry
They can't play an instrument
They can't be honest
Their words are neither
merciful nor wonderful
They speak meaninglessly
They walk with pride
All their actions are fraudulent
They all survive without satisfaction
What a load of crap!
Oh whatcha,
I decided to go back to my room
And I'm going to relax with a glass of tea
There are no questions or answers to their stupidity
I'm on my holiday
I need to honor myself

8. Stay Safe

I began the new chapter in my life with goodbye's
I am staying at home, staying safe
Each day
The ill cries that trouble my whole system
The thoughts that are hovering inside my brain
Lows and highs are like compressions and rarefactions in physics, which are seen on the oscilloscope
The eyes are not intended to shed tears, they are meant to shout
Shout for the truth and justice
The empty streets of my heart are like a half painting
But the wisdom is like bottle full of mineral water
I wish it would become a delicious wine
All I do is find time to eat
I get up late in the morning,
No time to exercise
Each day
I'm spinning all the time in relaxation
I examine myself, what makes life interesting?
Clock is ticking daily,
I should forget timepiece and have fun
I feel less at times when the world is too proud of its achievements

The holy sunlight sparkles during the dayspring
through the curtains of my corridor
The Golden Parakeet sings her heart out
Each day I assure myself that i will not be hypnotized by anyone's opinions
The long days of sleeping from morning to evening filled me with confidence
I evolved as a person through morning walks and nature's songs

9. Baby, I am going to get It

Baby I am going to get it
I just entered the mass hall
I fought the villains
I laughed at their jealousy
I wore a white tuxedo
I have bruises on my hands
Blood is coming from veins
When I sat for a while,
A boxing arm hit me hard,
My shoulder hit the ground
My teeth started showing blood
I laugh with blood on my teeth
Welcome to the bloody idiots who think they can ruin
Bloody No!
I am going to rule
Baby I am going to get it
I spied on their weapons and knives
Seeing those who are forthcoming to seize the treasure from me
I cried out, "Can you snatch my intelligence? Silly idiots"
I jumped to climb up
As the shaft of moonlight flashes,

I trashed all the nonsense into bin
I lack bullets in my gun, but I am the fire
I took off my hat to allow air
I used the rope to fly back and forth
I am paragliding in my dream world
Baby I am going to get it
I leaped across the walls
Getting best of the whole space with self faith
Acquiring treasures and powers
I skipped their blows
I stepped on their shoulders to reach my happiest place
I snugged the treasure trove
I closed the doors of this nothing left dynasty
I drove to a new place
To show my kindness
Baby I am going to get it

10. A Warrior

My eyes started bleeding
When I heard unsung songs
I walked in the deep forest, searching for ramen
I strolled around miles in the woods, looking around for water
I ambled right along the lake
I walked stealthily along with the wolves
I'm tired of searching for kindness!
Can we learn stillness from the river?
The search for mercy in the wild forest is similar
Forever in the jungle,
There is nothing that the forest cannot teach
Well, that's what I am gonna preach
I gathered firewoods and cooked ramen and drank water near the lake
I saw the Camaraderie of wolves and beasts in the jungle,
I can smell the stillness in hands of the wild forests
I was standing on the edge top of the mountain facing the sky
I call myself a winner
Bread winner, life winner
Unswerving kindness is paramount
Infact no one can mislead me
I'll keep walking and singing loudly

11. I saw you girl

I saw you girl
You look like a pearl
With spectacles
You sat with the other girls,
enduring their grim humor
That's not you
You were sitting quietly on the bench
The exciting part of you is somewhere
its deep, in the world of your own heart
I have entered your life
I feel your thoughts
I admire your cursive handwriting,
And Your fondness for simple things
Our sweet conversations
Little lovable mighty laughter
Your smile is a real fireside
Stood up and gave me warmth on my side
You made me realize
Your real eyes
I want to show you what love is
My kind of love is fathomless
I saw you girl
You look like a pearl

I offer my love to you
I incline towards you
We don't look at others
We don't listen to them
You showed me my grades through graphs
And we look at the graphs of fellow girl's graphs and giggle
Chemistry class that caused tension
bloomed the chemistry of our friendship's intention
The trigonometry we solved years ago
And yet, in life we face the same metrics to outgo
I perceived the true meaning of friendship
And forever we travel on the same ship
Its the twilight of the sky
I have had the same delight when I spoke to you again
I know you wrote letters for me
You know I wrote letters for you
You want love
I have it
The same light
We Shine brighter
I saw you girl
You look like a pearl

12. Give me some Tea

You want to oil your hair? Mom asked dad
I am hungry for Tea
"Good tea always enthralls us" Dad said
I know I know " Mumma said
"I love the gorgeous smell of it,
It is grown in the balcony of heavens
Brewed in the magic mountain water
The wonderful Tea is ready to drink after adding a little sugar
The best invention ever" exclaimed Dad with smile
Ah, ha ha I brought tea powder from the supermarket, boiled it with filter water" murmured Mumma
The magic in taste, the wonderful smell of the infusion is astonishing
I call Tea the "Medicine of relief"
That awesomeness vouchsafed me
The benefits of the tea though
It fills the void in stomach enough
Reinvigorates the mind
You will get the strength to climb the mountain
"Common, lets have some Tea" jumped Daddy with pleasure

13. Dog poem

Attaboy, Get a move on
Eat your kibble
Hurry up!
You'll need to undergo warm-up training
If you eat food, you will grow into a big doggy
You can heap, skip, hop, jog
You can find things with your scent
Quickly finish the food on your plate
Stop playing with critters
Allright, you're energetic creature
You might have to extend your limits,
determine to question your self-doubt
Growing up, you become a hunting Dog
Oh, my future wise trained good doggy
No one is concerned to teach you
You gotta learn for yourself
"Well Glad, you woke up darling"
How could you acknowledge all this at a tender age?
Imagine! You get a task of sniffing
Remember this, you must stalk swiftly on time being
You oughta make your master proud oneday

14. Life's a Cake

I am healthy
Happiness has nothing to do with being wealthy
Hip hip hurray
Ready for the day
Jumping everyday
Living near Amsterdam bay
Life is as good as you treat it
To eat a delicious piece, Bake it
Don't leave it half baked
All the goodness comes when ingredients are nicely cooked
You gotta use what you find
Learn to be kind
Find a comfy place to live
Life is like an ocean to dive
Take all that you get
Grab literally much of it

15. Breakthrough

I fight with myself everyday
To turn my weaknesses into strength
I'm looking at battlefield weapons
While the doors of insecurities open,
villians make silly chuckles
Asking to fight with open arms
The burning fires, boiling waters
The kingdom I was fighting for,
has already been conquered
I aint know this beforehand
In consideration of settling selfdoubt in combat
Although my brain always insisted not to sow the seeds of skepticism, the suspense of the battle survived
What exasperates me is, you cannot earn atleast a glass of water when you think enfeebled
I am the question,
I am the answer
I am the war
I have peace
No words, no mercy
There is no captaincy if you don't win
Start hunting like a lion

16. Don't need your review

Why do you preview?
I don't need your review
Am I not worth to read whole?
I perch and quiz myself
I wish you would read me
Acknowledge me
Why don't the forever's begin?
It doesn't matter you are right or wrong
I deserve the best no matter how cold the fight is
No matter how many times your belligerent doings crave for fight
I wish the shoulder and mind to be strong
I am a medalist of hardwork
I'm goodness in fairy tales
Just working for my words to spell out
I look forward to the fruits ripening, flowers blooming, nuts cracking, soul searching
I am loved by my faith
My laziness sings lullabies
I am competing with myself
In such a manner that I could adorn my enthusiasm

17. Bulky

You are the apple of my eye
Don't cut my feelings with lies
I am not the trouble that you underwent
I am the truth that you hunt
The smile on my teeth started hovering
When I get to know the feeling of leaving you in books of my dreams I was reading
Well you are unaware of that
I will do it without you qualifying
This is a great war to realize
My god is there for me to recognize
I built the walls of my empire with self-love
My attitude dictates them all

18. Wisp

We are misunderstood depending on where we live
We have built the gates of wisdom over years
Confidence is our shield
We refurbish ourselves to make our gardens grow in light forever
Ideas do not shine with age
Ideology of life shines when you illuminate your life on the path you walk with lamps of your knowledge

19. Wisdom

We grew up together as wild roses
nurtured ourselves in the snow
Smiling at the frost on the leaves
Sharing deep connections
stretching our branches, we grew taller
Over the wild winds
Basking in the rays of sunshine
Establishing each other's spirits in the storm
Inquisitively, travelling in the stream of life with distinctiveness
Whispering glitters of gold in the light
We are Growing forever in the forest of wisdom

20. Idea of life

I can handle life sitting in my room
Singing songs with plates and spoons as musical instruments,
Jumping and dancing with my weight
Lying on the floor,
Eating fruit salads is comfortable
The idea of cooking or organizing, working
it does not matter if I earn more than enough
on the flip side, the query of whether I can earn more than enough is peripheral
I got the answers
Life is not a treadmill
Some people imagine it is
They apply speed in their job, personal decisions and so on
All I wish in life is to enjoy its own favors

21. Work your guts out

Wow, I could see a bunch of eggplants in her bucket?
She collected from her vegetable garden
I repeated the same so that it could be heard by my mom
"Oh, stop that
Well don't think over and over about what others do
What should we do with their garden trees
Whether their plants will bear fruit,
Their tantrums are theirs
They are aware of their tricks
Why are you going nuts?" said mom
I want to grow our gardens the way they grow their gardens
Its amazing to see dozens and dozens of eggplants from their garden,
No pesticides sprinkled, harmless food, more natural produce
I believe that's the best way to eat, I said
"You just see the produce; have you ever noticed the difficulty they put into it?
It is not as easy as it seems, plants need to be raised like children
They should be protected from pest and insects,
watered every day, manured often to get the strength to bear fruit" says Mumma

"Woah, its like slogging guts out" I said "Its always better for us to do something for ourselves than to praise others deeds" I pondered

22. Slime

There is a crazy girl in the town
She wears a pink gown
She is passionate about making slime
She does that all the time
She says "Hurrah its breakfast time,
I will make a fluffy slime"
How about making it chocolate dip
Awe so smooth, do not touch it might slip
The fascinating mixture of foam and flour
Here goes in the orange food color
I will mix it up with zest of blueberry
The topping is the new Australian cherry

23. Pretty town

I taste the rainbows
The prettier rose grows
I touch the web of roses in a wild garden
I feel everything that a woman possibly can
I see the warmth of twilights
I feel each day is a Turkish delight
I smell the fragrance of flowers
And chirping of sparrows and cuckoos
How picturesque the mountains are
I would like to sit and stare
Walking down the pretty town road
I found sweet jumping little toad
The houses covered with mist
And bright flowers on the path that assist
It is a fantastic place to be

24. Bright Star

Universe
It is as beautiful as it is created
It is not affected as it appears
The twinkling stars shine on dark nights
everyday
stellar galaxies and their cosmic energies
work together to illuminate the bright light
Light that can be seen from an immense distance
the millions and trillions of stars are inspiring
Brace yourself, create what you can
Transform all your questions into energy
Bring out the inner energies of your soul
Be straightforward in what you can do
Take care of your own work

25. Be Still

Be still my dear soul
you grew up solving puzzles
people applauded when you received medal from
a freedom fighter
only then did you have decide to do something
for the nation
You trusted your heartbeats
and the blood in your veins,
the power of the soul
it will make you fly higher
The oceans that cross your heart,
The fears that engulf in your mind
They are like paper flies
you can deal with all of this
you are a wonderful thing
your cautiousness is your bling

26. Don't Listen to them

The entire crowd clamored
"Its your mistake,
you are not supposed to do this "
dont listen
You want to fly high
some external air tends to pull you down
Trying to keep your spirits under their control
dont listen
you are heading towards your dreams
they blabbered that it isn't virtuous method
if you listen to them, your dreams will become
dusted on the racks of your memory lane
dont listen
even the stars in the sky
May not be aware of their illuminous power
Yet people keep staring at the twinkling stars
with all the self belief, you can do it bigger
Those who humiliated you one day,
They will marvel at your good will

27. Rooster Morning

Good morning, Rooster
rolling over the stack of grass
she is a champion of eggs
what do you eat for breakfast?
you want to stroll into my plate of toast
go with a bag full of nuts
sprouts and butter nuts
huge vessel of varieties of cereals
you can also eat table scraps
you need a solid amount of healthy snacks
carrots and pumpkins
you want the entire world
or you want to be locked
my dear domestic friend,
to make our memories grand
rise and up again
loose some weight, that's a gain
weave a little more
start walking right here

Thanks To Lord Rama

Witness the mighty truth and hmmmmmmmmmm keep going.

9 798886 290332

Printed by Libri Plureos GmbH in Hamburg,
Germany